THE MEAN GIRLS

THE MEAN GIRLS
A Bunch of Bullies

Atiya C. Henley

Amyz Umbrella

Superior Publishing LLC.

This book is dedicated to all that have been bullied and are being bullied. Tell an adult! Don't try to fix it on your own. Tell until someone listens to you. You are beautiful and loved and there is nothing wrong with you, EXCEPT you're such an awesome person.

To ALL BULLIES
GET SOME HELP! YOU ARE JUST AS SPECIAL as everyone else. If you are hurt, don't hurt others.

Copyright © 2022 by Atiya C. Henley
Copyright © 2022 by Amyz Umbrella Pictures

All rights reserved. No part of this book may be reproduced in any manner whatsoever without written permission except in the case of brief quotations embodied in critical articles and reviews.

Superior Publishing LLC. 2022
Cedar Bluff, MS
662-295-9893

It was the first day of school and Layah was looking for her friend Maya. But she couldn't find her, Layah was so lonely.

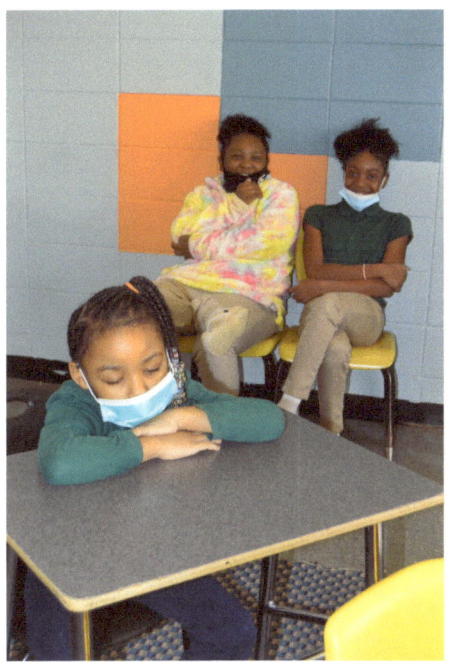

She walked into the classroom and the teacher told her to sit anywhere she wanted. So, she sat by her old crush named Dylan. She spoke and then after a while it was time to take attendance.

Mrs. Dawn, her teacher called their names and everyone answered, but when it got to Maya no-one answers, so she called the next person.

And then there was little knock at the door, So Mrs. Dawn told Alexa to open the door and there was Maya!

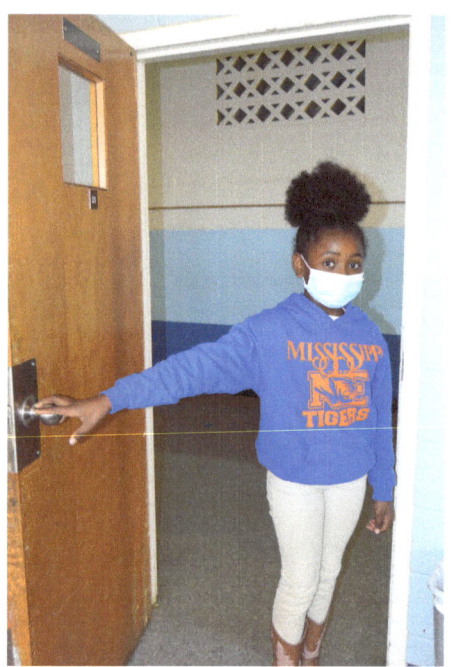

Maya said,

"I'm sorry I am late. I didn't wake up on time." Mrs. Dawn replied,

"It's okay this is a warning, but next time it's a tardy."
Maya thought to herself,

"Wow... what a great start for the first day!"

Today in Math they started long division. It was really hard. Layah was so confused, she asked for help but the teacher said,

"Not right now, use your smart little brain." That didn't help at all. She felt like someone watching her, then she heard them laugh.

She looked up and saw Alexa, Kayla and Siri they looked down hurriedly like they were not looking. She wondered, "Why were they laughing at her?" But she did not let it get to her.

The class went to lunch and Layah felt someone bumping into her. She turned and looked and they were laughing and pushing her. She yelled, "Stop it!" And they thought it was so funny so they started giggling and mocking her.

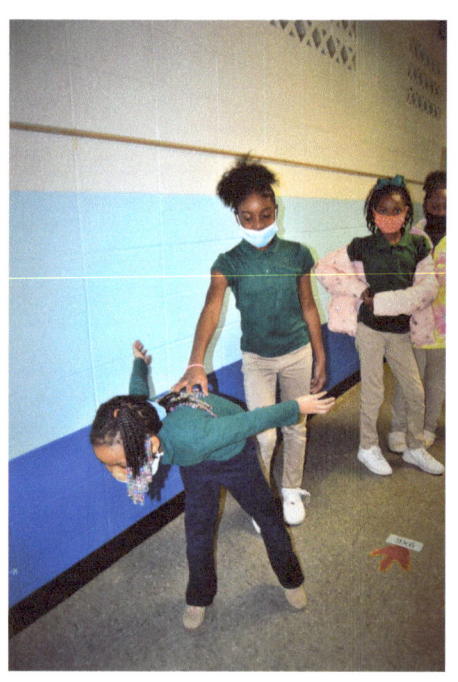

And then, they pushed her down. She was so hurt. She sat there in the hallway. No one helped her. They just pointed at her and laughed. Maya and Jade couldn't believe it.

She was so hurt and upset she sat with Maya and Jade. She told her best friends what was going on. Maya was upset. She told Layah they were just haters and just let them be her motivators!

They finished eating and went to play. They were having so much fun. And then Layah noticed that those mean girls were laughing loud and talking about someone. She didn't know if it was about her or someone else. So she tried to ignore them.

But then they came closer and closer to her and started saying, "Ugly ugly Layah!" Layah dropped her head and started to cry. Maya her bestie got angry, "Back off this little girl!" Maya was steaming hot. "Layah hasn't done anything to you! You want to mess with someone, MESS WITH ME!"

Maya was standing there with her fist balled, tears in her eyes and ready to fight.

Maya was standing there with her fist balled, tears in her eyes and ready to fight. She was tired of them messing with her best friend. They all started laughing, but walked away.

Layah looked up, "Thank you Maya cause you did not have to do that." They started playing again. Not long after that, it was time to go.

In the bathroom, all the mean girls were standing against the wall. Nobody was using it, they were just watching other girls come in so they could mess with them. Then their favorite person to mess with came in. When Layah walked in, Alexa pushed her, almost knocking her down. When she got up they all starting hitting her with wet paper towel.

But Layah was tired, she pushed Alexa back.

"I said to leave me alone! Stop messing with me!" Layah was angry. All the other girls ran out of the bathroom laughing.

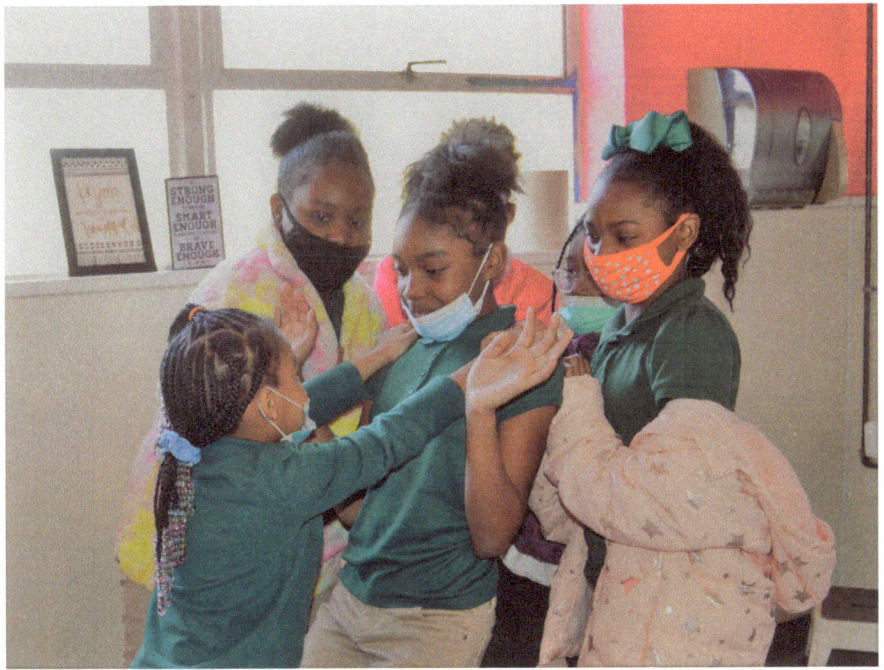

I HATE SCHOOL!

The next day Layah hated the thought of going back to school. Today she was on time, but when she got to class, the desks had been rearranged.

Guess who Layah had to sit next to? If you guessed Siri you are right.

All the mean girls were standing in front of Siri desk laughing.

Alexa pushed her. They all started to laugh. And then, Siri got up in her face after Alexa pushed her and called her a cry baby!

Alexa pushing Layah. What would you have done?

Layah was not going today, anger had taken over. Layah pushed Siri into the desk and she hit the floor. The other girls were shocked. But they still laughed at Layah and Siri.

But the teacher called Layah out, "Layah are you alright?"

Layah just shrugged her shoulders; she was just tired and miserable. The teacher asked Laylah out into the hallway. "Layah, I noticed that you've been acting kind of down lately.

Is everything okay at home?" The teacher grabbed Layah and looked into her face.

"Home is fine, but at school no!" The tears fell from Layah's eyes as she crossed her arms. Mrs. Dawn was worried,

"What is going on? You can tell me!" Mrs. Dawn noticed that this was really hurting Laylah.

"Siri, Kayla and Alexa mess with me every day. That's why I hate coming here! They laugh at me for no reason. They push me in the bathroom, in the lunch line, in the bus line, in the hallway. Everywhere I go they are there bullying me!" Laylah cried uncontrollably.

Mrs. Dawn was angry. She opened the classroom door as wide as it could go

"Siri, Kayla and Alexa out here now! Bullying will not be accepted in my classroom, in this school, nor in this world! It stops right now! Do you hear me?" Mrs. Dawn was yelling like a football coach.

"How does it feel to make someone cry for no reason? Make other kids not want to come to school and learn? All because you are being some MEAN GIRLS! TO THE OFFICE NOW!!!"

Maya stood up in the classroom and started to clap and the whole class stood up and clapped for Mrs. Dawn. They were all tired of the mean girls.

THE END!

FOR BULLIES AND THOSE BEING BULLIED

TO THE BULLY: Always remember you're gonna grow up and one day maybe have children and the Bible says what you do to others it will come back to you. This is something to think about before or if you are going down that road.

TO THE PERSON BEING BULLIED: If you are being bullied, most of the time you possess something that that person wants. Jealousy makes people dislike you for no reason but that doesn't mean that you have to take it, tell somebody until they listen. It's not your fault that you are loved and Special. Always remember it's not anything wrong with you it's something wrong with them

P.S. If mom and dad doesn't listen tell grandma she will come out of retirement!!!

Mrs. Frances, a Concerned Grandma

To the bully: I would say take a look at yourself. What is the real problem, because it's not me. To the victim: I would say as long as you love yourself never let anyone make you feel bad about yourself. You are beautiful/handsome, strong, courageous, smart, & blessed don't let anyone tell you different. Smile and continue with your day, never let anyone have that much power over you. We as parents and grandparents have start teaching our babies at home about self-love before the bullies gave a chance to tear them down.

Signed, forever in your corner with all love & gratitude, Catina

I like to say to a person that is bullied. You are not alone. There are people that love you. You are not alone. Talk to someone. We are here for you. Don't think that you have to deal with this alone. I'm always here for

you. There is nothing too hard for God. God said I will never leave you nor forsake you. I remembered when I use to be bullied growing up. I would stand up for myself. I was always encouraged to stand up for myself. But I had people that made a stand with me and for me. They had my back. They never left me. God will fight your battles for you. Never think that you have to end your life to be free. If you call on the name of the Lord. He will come. Talk to someone. That person that is bullying you is not worth losing your life over. There life is worthless and they probably want to be what you are. You are smart. You are beautiful. You are loved. Gods loves you and so do I. Reach out to someone. You are not alone.
Signed A Praying Preaching Police Named Robert

To the bully: I'm sorry that you weren't taught to love yourself a little more, but hurting others will never fill that void, only the love of God can when you let Him into your heart. Signed and Angel named Angelica

Stop! No one deserves to be treated this way! I know you can behave better than that! Mark 12:31, "Thou shalt love thy neighbor as thyself!"
Signed a Concerned Mother Clarissa

To the person being bullied... ask God to give you strength, stand your ground and the knowledge to know what to do when to do it. David was small but he won against Goliath the Giant. And, most importantly remember, Jesus will always be with you through every challenge; you're never alone.
Signed A Cool Cop that Preaches for Christ, Jeremy

To the Bully I am sorry for the trauma that you have endured that causes you to make others' lives miserable. Please put yourself in the spot of the person you're bullying, it doesn't feel good does it, so stop it now! To the one that's being bullied, I'm sorry that you were picked out to be pick on. They saw the greatness in you and tried to take it away but realized it wasn't as easy as it looked because greater is He that is in you than he that is in the world. I love you but God loves you more!
Signed A Caring Aunt and A Loving God Mother, Kay

As a therapist: A bully intent is always to threaten, insult, or harm someone who the bully feel is weaker or smaller than him or her. The bully also feels insecure about self & most of the time that's the reason for the bullying. So, I would say to the bully: STOP BULLYING ME (in an assertive way) I AM not afraid of you because I AM strong, I AM smart

& I AM a winner. You can also be kind like I am ....to treat others as you would like to be treated.

Signed A Caring Certified Therapist, Janice

Atiya is a 10 year old, fourth grader. She has a big heart and hates to see others hurt. She is passionate about taking care of others. She is currently working on other books. She would love to just give thanks to all of her classmates and their parents for allowing them to be apart of such an awesome accomplishment for her.

Thanks to the following students, teachers and principal.

Macaria, Erin, Kaylee, Kyleah, Azalea, Jayden, Braylen, Saniyah and her main character, and little cousin, Brandi.

Thanks to Principal Cox of West Clay Elementary for welcoming the idea, Coach Snow for allowing us to use his gym period and assisting in set-up, thanks to Mrs. Pumphrey for jumping in and being the courageous teacher.

Atiya would like to just thank you all for helping make one of her dreams come true.

www.ingramcontent.com/pod-product-compliance
Lightning Source LLC
Chambersburg PA
CBHW042300280426
43673CB00079BA/359